A Guide to the Cit

Birmingham is a modern and vibrant city. It has always been a city of change and currently much of its twentieth century architecture is giving way to new developments.

Exploring the two-hundred year old Georgian canal network and taking in Victorian and more recent street scenes brings the city's heritage to life. A visit to the Museum and Art Gallery gives a feel for the grand architectural ideals, while the Pre-Raphaelite art collection within gives an understanding of the artistic and social sides of Victorian life.

The ethos of today's city is founded on our forefathers' 'get on and do it' outlook on life. This is a centre for innovation and a dynamic hub of comme strongly supported by thr is a city full of exciting meeting, exhibition and sporting venues, and increasingly a 'must visit' place to shop.

Birmingham is a cosmopolitan city, respectful and inclusive of our many different cultures and lifestyles, and this brings a diverse and exciting side to today's Birmingham.

Understanding the city's past, and what is happening all around us today, is as relevant for those who have lived here all their lives as it is for Birmingham's increasing number of visitors and new residents. Greater appreciation of the city brings with it only positive ways forward.

Céline Gittens and Brandon Lawrence bring Birmingham Royal Ballet to Victoria Square as part of the Commonwealth Games handover.

The Library of Birmingham and Birmingham Rep, Centenary Square.

1

Earlier Times

Birmingham has grown from a medieval market centre. The oldest parts of the city centre are the Digbeth and Deritend areas, but wider Birmingham has developed out of some forty to fifty original hamlets and evidence of earlier life can be seen all over the city.

In the mid-12th century, Peter de Bermingham controlled the manor and was granted a market day which helped Birmingham become established as a trading centre. John Leland, a noted traveller in the reign of Henry VIII, visited Birmingham in 1538. He saw half-timbered houses and the parish church of St Martin, and noted that Birmingham was already involved in the metal trade, producing items such as knives and nails in small forges and workshops.

St Nicolas' Place in King's Norton is considered the finest collection of medieval buildings in Birmingham. It includes St Nicolas' Church, a Tudor Merchant's House (above) and the Old Grammar School (below).

The Staffordshire Hoard is the largest collection of Anglo-Saxon gold ever found. It was discovered in a field north of Birmingham by a metal detectorist and is on display in the Birmingham Museum and Art Gallery.

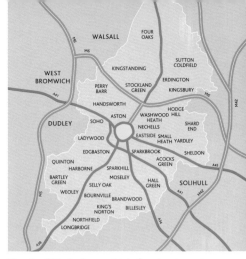

The city of Birmingham as it is today, showing main roads and motorways.

Interestingly, Birmingham itself initially lacked the natural resources or geographical position to promote early growth. However, raw materials were to be found just to the north-west in the Black Country, an area rich in coal, iron-ore and lime. At first, the metal-working industry had to depend on power from water wheels. Later, steam engines provided more reliable power while the spread of canal transportation led to much cheaper coal, giving a competitive advantage to Birmingham manufacturers.

Birmingham Town Hall was constructed from 1834. It has seen some historic musical landmarks, including the premières of Mendelssohn's Elijah in 1846 and Elgar's The Dream of Gerontius in 1900.

Back to Back Houses, Hurst Street. A court of early 19th Century dwellings, each decorated in different period styles. A popular attraction run by the National Trust.

3

Aston Hall is to be found close to the A38(M). With its splendid Long Gallery (above), it is one of the hidden delights of Birmingham.

Aston Hall and the Cathedrals

Many large English country houses were built in Warwickshire in the late sixteenth and early seventeenth centuries. An excellent example is Aston Hall, a fine Jacobean manor, now a museum run by Birmingham Museums.

Birmingham's Anglican Cathedral is an example of the work of architect Thomas Archer, with fine Roman Baroque detail, especially in the concave tower.

Not far away is the Roman Catholic St Chad's Cathedral, designed by A.W.N. Pugin, the leading architect of the Gothic revival.

St Philip's Cathedral was consecrated as a church in 1715 and became a cathedral in 1905.

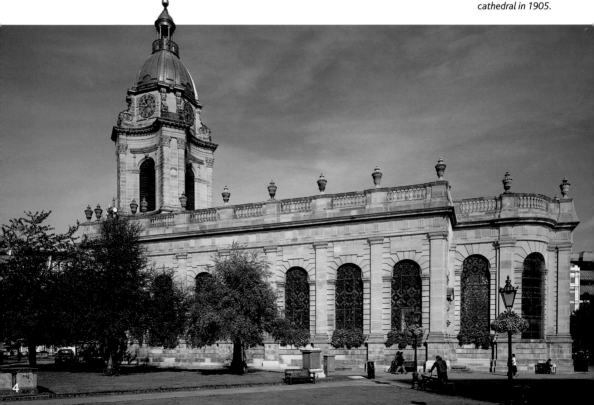

Boulton, Watt & Murdoch

The Industrial Revolution of the 18th century was a time of tremendous activity in Birmingham. Many entrepreneurs contributed to the growth of industry but none was more famous than the partnership of Matthew Boulton and James Watt, in which William Murdoch also played an important part.

Matthew Boulton was the son of a Birmingham silver stamper and piercer, making small metal items known as 'toys'. On the death of his father, Matthew took over the business and set about manufacturing on a grand scale. He had considerable entrepreneurial spirit and was keenly aware of the need for commercial tools such as market research, public relations and marketing, and of the importance of political contacts – nothing changes! Boulton set out to produce high quality products and he invested in the best workers to help in developing his large-scale industrial operations.

The Smethwick Engine. This 1778 Boulton & Watt engine was used to pump water back up the canal locks at Smethwick from 1779 until 1891.

Water mills, such as Sarehole Mill in Hall Green, were important for power. The writer J.R.R. Tolkien once lived close by. Here he got inspiration for the mill and village in The Hobbit.

Power for the World

Matthew Boulton established the Soho Manufactory at Handsworth Heath, just north of Birmingham. The manufactory was completed in the early 1770s. Initially, water-wheels provided power for manufacturing, but as production increased their limited output became a serious problem. The solution was found when James Watt came to join Boulton in partnership at Soho from 1774. Steam engine design and manufacture became a major part of the work of the firm of Boulton & Watt, including the assembly of pumping engines to help keep the Cornish tin and copper mines dry.

Some Lost Opportunities

Central to the installation of steam engines in Cornwall was William Murdoch, who joined the firm in 1777. Murdoch had travelled from Ayrshire to seek work at Soho. Boulton was so impressed with the workmanship of a wooden hat, which Murdoch had turned on a home-made lathe, that he employed him. For many years Murdoch worked for Boulton and Watt in Cornwall. During his stay in Redruth, Murdoch became very interested in producing a steam carriage. Indeed, he made working models, but the firm did not back his invention. Murdoch also invented gas lighting, although sadly he failed to obtain a patent for it. The Soho Manufactory offices were lit by gaslight and the firm became involved in the manufacture of gas-making equipment.

Soho House was the home of Matthew Boulton and is now a museum. It is a fitting place to learn more about the partnership of Boulton & Watt, and the Lunar Society.

The Soho Manufactory was situated just down the hill from Soho House.

The model steam carriage built by William Murdoch while in Redruth, Cornwall.

The Lunar Society Room at Soho House. This is the original table that the group met around.

The Lunar Society

The Industrial Revolution was aided by the exchange of ideas among a number of philosophical groups. The Lunar Society was one such group, of which Boulton and Watt were key members. Indeed, Soho House, the home of Boulton, was often the meeting place of the group, so-named because they met at the time of the full moon to illuminate their journey home.

Other leading figures in the group included Josiah Wedgwood of pottery fame, Joseph Priestley, discoverer of oxygen, and William Withering who extracted digitalis from the foxglove and used it in the treatment of heart conditions. These are just a few of the influential members, eleven of whom became Fellows of the Royal Society.

The Lunar Society existed between 1766 and 1809 and its success lay in the varying professional backgrounds of the membership and their different approaches to the topics under discussion.

Boulton, Watt & Murdoch (William Bloye, 1956) will be a major feature of the redevelopment of Centenary Square.

Jewellery Quarter

The Birmingham Jewellery Quarter is situated just a few minutes walk from the city centre. It is a major centre for the modern day jewellery business, and of considerable interest for its industrial architecture, general ambience, and for modern-day city living.

The jewellery industry relies on a large number of specialist skills with part-finished items being transferred between different craftsmen, who usually work in close proximity.

The Quarter became established when the Colmore family sold plots of land for building in the eighteenth century with Birmingham 'toy' makers soon moving into the houses. A second area of land was released in the nineteenth century and again residential houses were converted and extended into business premises with many 'pegs' (small workshop areas) available for rent by artisans. The survival of the Birmingham Jewellery Quarter

through various recessions has been helped by the considerable infrastructure that built up around the industry. This has included the Assay Office, bullion dealers, local engineering expertise, the establishment of the School of Jewellery, which is now part of Birmingham City University, and the ready availability of gas supplies.

St Paul's Square

St Paul's is the last remaining Georgian square in the city, with the elegant church of St Paul's at its centre. Both Matthew Boulton and James Watt had pews in the church, though their family church, where they are both buried, is St Mary's in Handsworth.

St Paul's Square.

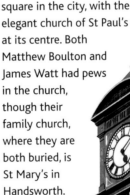

The Chamberlain Clock in the centre of the Jewellery Quarter commemorates the association with Joseph Chamberlain who represented the area as an MP.

The Conversion of St Paul *(Francis Eginton, 1791) is a fine painted window. Today, St Paul's Church is the venue for many types of concert – here Sing! Bentley Heath entertain.*

St Paul's Church was designed by Roger Eykyn and dates from 1779.

Assay Office

Matthew Boulton was instrumental in the opening of the Assay Office in 1773. His business was hindered by having to send items to Chester for hallmarking and he successfully petitioned parliament for the establishment of the Birmingham office. Of course it was Boulton who was the first to send items for assay when the original office opened above the King's Head public house in New Street. Today the Birmingham Assay Office is the busiest in the United Kingdom.

The Anchor Town Mark forms part of the hallmark on items assayed by the Birmingham office.

Jewellery Workshop, Warstone Lane: Rob Turley is a traditional jewellery craftsman who produces original work and also undertakes alterations and repairs for the trade and the public.

The Museum of the Jewellery Quarter

The old Smith and Pepper works has been turned into the Museum of the Jewellery Quarter. This traditional Jewellery Quarter business closed in 1981 and the premises have been preserved just like a giant 'time capsule'.

The museum includes tours and resident jewellers who discuss their work with visitors. The centre also has an excellent retail outlet for the work of local jewellers.

The Museum of the Jewellery Quarter.

School of Jewellery, Birmingham City University. Traditional 'peg' style benches are available to students 12 hours a day.

Traditional 'peg' preserved at the Museum of the Jewellery Quarter.

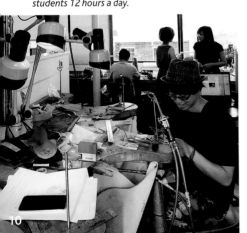

The Argent Centre, built for the firm of W.E. Wiley, employed 250 people in pen production. Today, it provides units for industrial and commercial use and is home to the Pen Museum.

Modern Jewellery Quarter

The 'urban village' concept has seen major developments in today's Jewellery Quarter with a number of former industrial premises converted into fine residential accommodation. The number of people living here is rising towards 10,000 and they co-exist with successful companies working in traditional jewellery industries, alongside many other businesses.

Newman Brothers Coffin Fitting Works. This factory closed in 1999. It produced brass and plated coffin fittings, including those for the Royal Family. A fascinating museum close to the city centre.

Canal City

The canals of Birmingham and the Black Country.

Today, the city centre canal network is incorporated into modern redevelopments. The system is a reminder of Georgian industrialisation, right in the heart of the modern city. Original canal construction took place from the mid-eighteenth century, with most of the main canals being completed by the early 1800s. These man-made waterways were vital for the carriage of raw materials and finished goods, and stimulated rapid industrial development. When the canal from the Wednesfield coalfield in the Black Country reached Birmingham in 1769, the price of coal fell by 50% overnight.

Early Canal Improvements

The original route from the Black Country to Birmingham was surveyed by the great canal builder James Brindley, but by the 1820s this canal was not coping with the large volume of traffic. Thomas Telford was asked to survey the canal and he reported that it had become "little better than a crooked ditch". His recommendations included straightening and widening the canal, and reducing the number of locks. Edgbaston Reservoir was also built to improve the canal's water supply.

Gas Street Basin, where the Birmingham Canal Navigation and the Worcester and Birmingham Canal meet.

The Guillotine Lock at King's Norton. The lock marks the junction of the Worcester & Birmingham and Stratford Canals. It maintained a six inch difference in water level between the two canals right up until canal nationalisation in 1948.

A Georgian canal bridge (below left) is used by conference delegates to transfer between the Convention Centre and Arena Birmingham.

The International Convention Centre (below right) is a major meeting venue.

Arena Birmingham on the canal edge by Old Turn Junction is a major sporting and concert venue. It also provides an exhibition space for major meetings held at the International Convention Centre close-by.

Sherborne Wharf (below) is a canal loop formed when the canal was straightened by Thomas Telford in the 1820s and is now a popular place for city living.

Much of Brindley's winding Old Main Line still exists, forming interesting loops to explore.

Canal Heritage Today

Birmingham is now making excellent use of its canal heritage. This can be seen on a large scale at Brindleyplace. Here the 200 year old canal is now fronted with new offices and housing developments, as well as leisure and entertainment venues.

On the opposite bank are the International Convention Centre and Birmingham Arena. Nearby is the National Sea Life Centre. Canal-based walking routes are increasingly linking major regional centres in the Midlands and there is a Birmingham to London long-distance walk along the Grand Union Canal.

The National Sea Life Centre offers a very different kind of city living for these penguins.

Victorian Ideals

The Victorian period was a time of considerable activity and immense change in Birmingham. With flourishing industries of every description, Birmingham became known as the 'town of a thousand trades' and experienced tremendous growth in population as people moved from rural areas to seek work. This rapid expansion also brought with it considerable problems of poor quality housing and public health.

The 'Civic Gospel'

In 1854, a young man named Joseph Chamberlain came to work for his uncle's screw-making firm Nettlefold. The firm became very successful, making wood screws by a new process, and Chamberlain had time to look around and consider the problems in the town. He was encouraged by the 'Civic Gospel' ideas that people should take greater responsibility for such things as education, living and working conditions. Indeed, it became clear that the future success of this now great town depended on a major improvement of the municipal infrastructure.

The Memorial Fountain in Chamberlain Square (John H Chamberlain, 1880) with the Museum and Art Gallery (Yeoville Thomason, 1885) behind.

Terracotta Everywhere!

When Joseph Chamberlain became Mayor in 1873, he set out his aims for radical improvement, promising that the town "shall not, with God's help, know itself!". Birmingham set to work on some enormous projects that aroused interest across Europe. The Council's purchase of the two gasworks and the waterworks in the town brought in considerable revenue. This helped to finance some of their major programmes for improving public health, education and living conditions. Schools and libraries were built, a sewage system installed, and ultimately water was brought from the Elan Valley in mid-Wales. Large municipal projects were also undertaken in the town: the new Council House and Law Courts were constructed and Corporation Street developed as a grand commercial area in the centre of Birmingham. Many of the schools and libraries built at this time survive across today's city as reminders of a period of dynamic change.

George Dawson was a preacher of the 'Civic Gospel' which fired-up Joseph Chamberlain and his contemporaries into radical action.

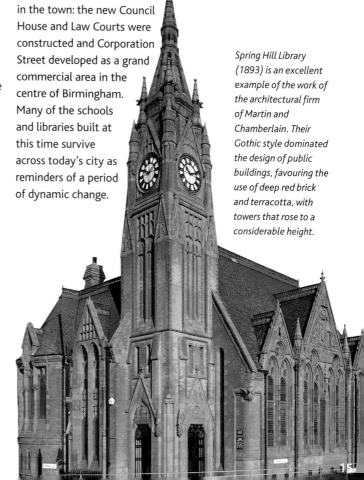

Spring Hill Library (1893) is an excellent example of the work of the architectural firm of Martin and Chamberlain. Their Gothic style dominated the design of public buildings, favouring the use of deep red brick and terracotta, with towers that rose to a considerable height.

The Victoria Law Courts (Aston Webb and Ingress Bell, 1887-91) on Corporation Street demonstrates intricate use of terracotta design.

The characteristic building material of the late Victorian era was terracotta, which was used both internally and externally. Terracotta is usually coloured red or buff and is a hard-wearing, moulded clay building material which allows intricate detailing, while being extremely resistant to a dirty industrial environment. There are many fine examples of terracotta

The School of Art (Martin & Chamberlain, 1885) is a fine example of late Victorian red brick and terracotta and today is part of the Birmingham City University Faculty of Arts, Design and Media.

buildings to be found in the city, often in the Victorian Gothic style advocated by John Ruskin.

Victoria Square is the municipal heart of the city, surrounded by the 1874 Council House and other notable buildings. Works by Dhruva Mistry make up a major art installation. Due to leaks in The River water feature this is currently filled with pot plants, courtesy of the city's parks department.

Edwardian Swimming Lives On

Moseley Road Baths (Cossins and Peacock , 1907)

Moseley Road Baths in Balsall Heath was saved from closure in 2017. Campaigning groups persuaded the Council to allow the baths to be kept open. A local Community Interest Company will now run the baths. Work with heritage organisations has secured over a million pounds to ensure the baths are retained for all to enjoy in the longer term, but ultimately the baths will rely on members of the public using them to ensure that they can continue to be enjoyed by future generations.

The steam-heated towel drying racks are still in place.

The Second Class Baths are open for public swimming and are an amazing experience.

The Gala Pool – this was the First Class Baths, but is not currently available to swim in!

The Library of Birmingham

The Library of Birmingham is not only Europe's largest regional library and a must-visit spot for locals, but also a significant tourist attraction for visitors, as well as being a place in which many choose to study. It was conceived as a 'people's palace' and its close proximity to the Jewellery Quarter influenced its circular design theme. Who said public libraries have had their time!

The Shakespeare Memorial Room was originally housed in the 1879 Victorian library and is now in the golden oval space on the top floor.

The Library of Birmingham (Francine Houben, 2013) has many circular design elements, here extended to the lighting.

Asymmetric floor stacking allows two levels of gardens which offer great views of the redeveloping city.

Art for All

Birmingham has often incorporated significant public art projects into redevelopments.

As a city founded on the huge efforts of Victorian entrepreneurs, it is fitting that the Museum and Art Gallery holds the world's largest collection of Pre-Raphaelite artworks. A huge figure in the second wave of the Pre-Raphaelite movement was Sir Edward Burne-Jones, who was born in Bennett's Hill in the centre of Birmingham. In his later years, Burne-Jones produced designs for stained glass windows in St Philip's Cathedral.

In the Digbeth and Deritend areas there is now an emphasis on graffiti street art, although there is perhaps a delicate balance to be drawn between encouraging appropriate artworks without allowing an open-house for spraying 'tags' all over the built environment.

The Nelson Monument *(Sir Richard Westmacott, 1809) is the oldest public art on the streets of Birmingham.*

The Last of England *(Ford Maddox-Brown, 1855) is a highly regarded painting in the Pre-Raphaelite collection at Birmingham Museum and Art Gallery.*

The Last Judgement *(Sir Edward Burne-Jones for Morris & Co, 1896). One of the last church window designs Burne-Jones undertook, and considered one of his finest.*

Wattilisk *(Vincent Woropay, 1988)* is located outside the Queen Elizabeth II Law Courts and illustrates a James Watt invention for replicating sculptures at different sizes.

Guardian Sphinx *(Dhruva Mistry, 1993)* is part of a major installation in Victoria Square.

Inside Tempus Fugit *(Ray Lonsdale, 2004). The head alludes to the idea that 'no man can escape the nine-year old boy he once was' and is positioned outside Aston University Library.*

Sentinel *(Tim Tolkien, 2000)* is to be found outside the Castle Bromwich factory where Spitfires were built in World War II.

A Supermarine Mark IX Spitfire at Thinktank, Birmingham Science Museum.

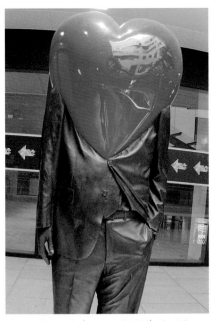

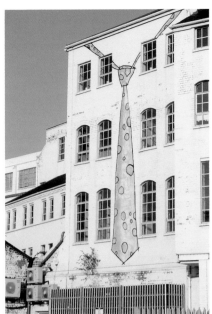

The Lovely People (*Arron Bird, 2010*), *The Cube*.

Street graffiti art is to be found around every corner in Digbeth and Deritend.

On the Stage

Birmingham has made a major contribution to the arts. From the huge influence of Black Sabbath to the Rock Music sound of the 1960s and the setting up of the Repertory Theatre by Sir Barry Jackson, through to the amazing, inclusive approach of the Birmingham Opera Company today.

Symphony Hall is the home of the City of Birmingham Symphony Orchestra, which has a world-renowned reputation. The hall itself has a radical adjustable acoustic design and is considered among the best concert venues in the world.

Birmingham Royal Ballet came to the city in 1990 and, from their home at Birmingham Hippodrome, established themselves as a leading company.

Birmingham Royal Ballet perform The Nutcracker, *a popular production often staged coming up to Christmas. David Bintley has been the hugely successful Artistic Director since 1995 and will retire in July 2019.*

The CBSO at Symphony Hall. Andris Nelsons' farewell concert with the CBSO who, together with the CBSO Choruses, performed Mahler's Symphony No. 3.

Today, many smaller venues in the city and suburbs give a platform for the latest bands and there is always plenty of theatre to experience.

The Notebenders can be found performing free on Saturday lunchtimes in Symphony Hall Café.

The Birmingham Jazz & Blues Festival takes place each July in venues across Birmingham, Solihull and Sandwell.

The innovative Birmingham Opera Company stages large-scale productions in unique locations. They regularly feature volunteer performers from the Birmingham community.

Twentieth Century Architecture

O n occasion we can be too close to something to fully appreciate it and arguably this is true of the attitude of many of us to the 'brutalist' concrete architecture with which much of Birmingham was rebuilt after World War II.

A lot has now been demolished, some controversially, however there is plenty still to consider and by creating interest it is more likely that the best will survive.

In particular there are several artworks by William Mitchell in the city which are little known but well worth exploring, including a series of concrete art installations on a John Madin office block in Broad Street and huge installations in a subway underneath Hockley Flyover.

Concrete panel (William Mitchell, 1965), on Quayside Tower, Broad Street.

New Street signal box (Bicknell & Hamilton and W. R. Healey, 1964). This 'brutalist' design houses once state-of-the-art equipment and is still in use today.

The Climbing Frame
(*William Mitchell,
1968*). *The subway
entrance under
Hockley Flyover is
decorated with one of
Mitchell's 'poured in
situ' concrete artworks,
which has worn well.*

*The Rotunda (James
Roberts, 1965)
remains from the
1960s Bull Ring
shopping centre.*

*Spaghetti Junction is
perhaps the ultimate
icon to Birmingham's
1970s concrete
architectural design.*

Industry & Commerce

Historically known as the 'town of a thousand trades' and with an emphasis on engineering and metal-working, today's city now has an increasingly mixed economy, including new high technology industries. Birmingham is growing in strength as a commercial centre, especially in banking, and also as a primary retail destination.

Cars into the Future

After some difficult times, the car industry in Birmingham has seen a resurgence. Jaguar Land Rover have key production plants in the West Midlands, including the Lode Lane factory in Solihull, the home of the Range Rover, and the Jaguar factory in Castle Bromwich.

The Birmingham car industry's history goes back to 1895, when Fred Lanchester produced the first four-wheel, petrol-driven car. Later, Herbert Austin's company developed into a pioneer of mass-production, driven forward by

important engineering breakthroughs. The Austin Seven was Britain's first mass-produced car and in the 1960s the Mini had both revolutionary front-wheel drive and a transverse-mounted engine. Today, research and development is focusing on products for tomorrow's world, such as driverless cars and fully electrically powered vehicles.

The Austin Seven fulfilled the ambition of Herbert Austin to "motorise the masses". Stanley Edge was the young designer for this car. Approximately 300,000 were built between 1922 and the Second World War.

Jaguar Land Rover produce a successful range of luxury cars including the Solihull born Range Rover (below) and the Castle Bromwich built F-Type sports car (left).

Deutsche Bank trading floor at their Brindleyplace headquarters.

Banking Centre

The depth of commercial investment is emphasised by HSBC's decision to relocate their national headquarters for retail banking to Birmingham. Their prestigious new Broad Street main offices will open in 2019. Of course a number of high street banks started here in Birmingham, including Lloyds, TSB and HSBC, which grew out of the Midland Bank, whose former headquarters is now the Apple Store in New Street.

Exhibitionists!

The NEC opened in 1976 and is a leading event and exhibition centre which hosts events such as Crufts. Nearby, Birmingham Airport offers a convenient gateway to the world with direct flights to major cities and world hubs, while Resorts World adds a mix of leisure and entertainment activities to the area.

Long-haul flights out of Birmingham Airport.

Resorts World adds a mix of leisure and entertainment activities.

The NEC hosts many prestigious events.

The Mailbox canalside.

Retail Therapy

In the Victorian era, Birmingham knew the importance of retail. This included the grand Corporation Street which replaced areas of poor quality housing. Today, the 'shopping experience' provided by Birmingham city centre is substantial: from Bullring, Grand Central and five department stores, through to high-end offerings in The Mailbox, together with many other shopping locations. The impact of the current conversion of the Pavilions Shopping Centre into the 'largest Primark in the world' should not be underestimated!

Piccadilly Arcade off New Street started life as a picture house, before being converted to retail in 1926. In 1989, intriguing trompe l'oeil 3-D ceiling paintings were added by artist Paul Maxfield.

The Wholesale Markets currently supply the Bullring Retail Market close to St Martin's Church.

Great Western Arcade is built over Snow Hill railway tunnel.

City Life

Birmingham has a surprising number of parks and public places and there is lots to see and do. The city has three universities and a very large student population. The University of Birmingham is situated in leafy Edgbaston, the Aston University campus is close to the city centre, and Birmingham City University is increasingly based at Eastside.

Diverse Cultural Backgrounds

Many Birmingham people are descended from previous generations who came to the city in search of work and a more prosperous life. This is true of the many migrants from Wales and Ireland as

The Botanical Gardens in Edgbaston is just one of many green spaces in the city.

St Patrick's Day celebrations (left) centre on the Irish Quarter in Digbeth. Here the Birmingham Irish Pipes and Drums pass the Old Crown pub, the only timber-framed medieval building left in Deritend.

Eid Prayers in Small Heath Park (above) are one of a number of open air events to observe the Eid ul-Fitr Prayer.

The Vaisakhi Festival includes a procession which ends with celebrations in Handsworth Park.

A Bhangra masterclass at Birmingham Rep (left).

Each September, Carnival brings a giant Caribbean party to Birmingham (right).

Frankfurt Christmas Market is a huge attraction in the city.

well as those from areas of the Commonwealth such as the West Indies and Asia. Birmingham presently has the largest ethnic minority population of any city in the United Kingdom. This wide diversity of cultural backgrounds adds new dimensions to Birmingham life. The City Council works hard to ensure that people understand and appreciate the different cultures around them. Chinese New Year is celebrated in style in the Chinese Quarter, close to the Hippodrome. In a similar way other religious festivals are properly recognised in various parts of the city.

Birmingham Pride takes to the streets each May with a spectacular carnival procession followed by a weekend festival centred in the Gay Village around Hurst Street.

Cannon Hill parkrun. Runners pass the Golden Lion, originally a sixteenth century guild house in Deritend, which was moved to its current location due to road widening.

Birmingham Great Run. This half Marathon is held annually in October. As a warm-up, why not consider the Birmingham 10k in late spring?

Dragon Race sees Birmingham businesses compete to see who can paddle fastest along the canals.

Balti and More

Birmingham is the home of Balti cooking. A Balti is literally a metal dish, similar to a wok, in which a Balti curry is served. It is usually accompanied with naan or chapati rather than rice and is washed down with a beverage brought in by the customer. The Balti style of food is thought to originate from Kashmir, though many would say its true home is the Sparkbrook and Balsall Heath area of Birmingham! Balti Houses or Sweet Centres, so called because they also sell Asian sweets, are now found all over the city and are imitated in every corner of the United Kingdom and abroad. For the truly authentic Balti taste and atmosphere the restaurants on Ladypool Road and Stoney Lane in Sparkhill take some beating.

Adil balti house in Stoney Lane, Sparkhill.

Aston Villa host West Bromwich Albion at Villa Park.

Sport in the City

There are three first-class football teams associated with the city, Birmingham City based at St Andrew's, Aston Villa at Villa Park, and West Bromwich Albion at The Hawthorns. All three teams play exciting football in modern stadiums and have considerable followings in the city.

The home of Warwickshire Cricket Club is in Edgbaston. Cricket has been played at the County Ground for over a hundred years. Edgbaston is often the venue for an England Test Match in the summer.

Edgbaston Cricket Ground is the home of Warwickshire County Cricket Club.

21st Century Birmingham

Landmark developments of recent times have included the opening of the ICC & Symphony Hall in the early 1990s and the new Bullring in 2003. Projects in Eastside created Millennium Point, now surrounded by the relocated faculties of Birmingham City University. The major refurbishment of New Street Station, with the Grand Central retail centre above, was completed in 2015. The long-term objectives of breaching the constraining 1960s inner ring road and creating a significant pedestrian ribbon through the city are gradually being achieved.

Urban Paradise

On into the future, 'Paradise' in Chamberlain Square is a redevelopment of the space formerly occupied by the Central Library complex, while the Arena Central project, adjacent to Broad Street, is a mixed-used area which will include the new national headquarters of HSBC Retail Banking. In 2018, several high rise developments were begun, including 103 Colmore Row, due to open for business in 2020, where a new skyscraper will replace the John Madin designed NatWest Tower. In Digbeth, close to the Bullring, the Beorma Quarter development will add a very futuristic feel, promising spectacular views from its 'sky garden'.

High Speed Two

The success of Birmingham's city centre projects has seen many more people coming to work in the city. Public transport improvements include the extension of the tram system from Grand Central on to Broad Street and then to Five Ways. Work has now started on the

Chamberlain Square. The final demolition stages of John Madin's 1960s Central Library complex reveals an amazing vista.

Birmingham Curzon Street terminal for High Speed Two, close to Millennium Point. This will incorporate the original Curzon Street Station frontage into a modernistic design. As part of this project, the HS2 offices have moved to the city, a number of engineering companies are expanding their presence in Birmingham, and a National College for High Speed Rail has been opened alongside the canal by Aston University.

For green transport, significant investment in canal towpaths sees an increasing number of commuters cycling to work along the canal system.

Wholesale Demolition

Many other developments are planned, including demolition of the Wholesale Markets to the south of the city centre. The area around Snow Hill Station and the Aston end of Corporation Street, including the Central Methodist Hall and Victoria Law Courts, will all feature in future plans.

Live, Work and Play!

Birmingham has taken a long-term view of redevelopment. The city has faced up to the decline of its dominant manufacturing sector with plans to broaden the city's economic base. When considered together, recent projects are beginning to seem as significant for the city as those of Joseph Chamberlain's era.

All this bodes well for one of Europe's youngest workforces who enjoy many opportunities in a city in which it is great fun to live, work and play!

The Birmingham 2022 Commonwealth Games will bring a focus on the city's sporting activities in the next four years.

Canal towpaths radiating out from the city centre have had millions of pounds spent to provide safer cycle commuting.

Birmingham's National College for High Speed Rail uses an ex-Eurostar Class 373 power car for virtual reality training in preparation for the opening of the HS2 line.

Work soon starts on the Birmingham HS2 terminus which will incorporate Curzon Street Station.

Things to do in Birmingham

Here are ideas for things to see and do in Birmingham and the surrounding area. Basic details are given here with further information on the sister website, including links to venue websites with full details of opening times and prices. For those of you settling in to Birmingham the website also gives further details on many aspects of city life.

CITY CENTRE ATTRACTIONS

Fold out the cover to see the map>

Arcadian
Entertainment and party venue in Chinatown – Map F6

Arena Birmingham
Sporting and concert venue – Map A4

Back to Backs
Surviving back to back court houses and a key attraction – Map E6

BBC
Tour of BBC Birmingham at Mailbox – Map D6

Birmingham Hippodrome
Home of Birmingham Royal Ballet and hosts wide variety of performances – Map E6

Birmingham Museum and Art Gallery
World's largest collection of pre-Raphaelite artworks – Map D4

Birmingham REP
Longest-established of Britain's building-based theatre companies – Map C4

Blue Orange Theatre
Independent theatre in Birmingham's Jewellery Quarter – Map C1

Bullring & Grand Central
Shopping destinations with over 200 stores – Map F5, E5

Canal Boat Trips
Canal tours leave from the back of the ICC and from Gas St. Basin – Map B5

CBSO Centre
Practice and concert venue – Map C6

Crescent Theatre
A wide range of drama and music productions – Map A5

Custard Factory
Creative and digital businesses, independent shops and venues – Map H6

Electric Cinema
Oldest working cinema in the world – Map E6

Five Ways Leisure Complex
Mixed leisure – Map A6

Gay Village
Adjacent to the Chinese Quarter around Hurst Street – Map E6

Glee Club
Comedy club and music venue staging regular stand-up nights – Map F6

Ikon Gallery
Modern art gallery in an historic Martin & Chamberlain board school – Map B5

Legoland Discovery Centre
Adults must be accompanied by a child! – Map A5

Library of Birmingham
Europe's largest public library with viewing gardens – Map C4

Mailbox
Stylish shopping, lifestyle & restaurant destination, including exclusive stores – Map C6

Museum of the Jewellery Quarter
Preserved factory with guided tours and retail area – Map B1

National Sea Life Centre
Over 60 displays of freshwater and marine life – Map B5

New Alexandra Theatre
Often known as 'the Alex' dating from 1901 and in an art deco style – Map E6

Newman Brothers Museum/Coffin works
Explores social history and cultural change through the eyes of a Jewellery Quarter firm – Map C4

O2 Academy
Music venue – Map E7

Old Joint Stock Theatre
Studio theatre with new plays, musical theatre, comedy improv – Map E4

Old Rep
First purpose-built repertory theatre – Map E5

Parkside Gallery
Exhibitions from acclaimed artists and designers – Map H3

Pen Museum
Based in a former pen factory in the heart of Birmingham's Jewellery Quarter – Map B3

Piccadilly Arcade
Shopping arcade which Includes Trompe l'oeil 3-D illusional ceiling art – Map E5

Positively Birmingham Walking Tours
Guided tours of the city centre, weekends and some weekdays – Map C5, D4

RBSA Gallery
Royal Birmingham Society of Artists gallery – Map C3

Spring Hill Library
Community library designed by Martin and Chamberlain – Map A3

St Chad's Cathedral (RC)
Significant Augustus Pugin architecture – Map E2

St Martin in the Bull Ring
Parish church of Birmingham. 1876 Burne-Jones/Morris window – Map F5

St Philip's Cathedral (CofE)
Baroque church with stained glass by Sir Edward Burne-Jones – Map E4

Symphony Hall
Home of the City of Birmingham Symphony Orchestra – Map B5

Thinktank, Birmingham Science Museum
Contains oldest working James Watt steam engine in the world – Map G4

Town Hall
Concert and event venue – Map D4

Two Towers Brewery
Local brewery with tours – Map E2

Victoria Law Courts
A functioning magistrate's court – Map F3

Walk of Stars
Famous names from popular culture along Broad Street – Map C5-B6

www.discoveringbirmingham.co.uk